You Can't
Win
a Fight
with
Your Client

You Can't
Win
a Fight
with
Your Client

& 49 Other
Rules for
Providing
Great Service

TOM MARKERT

Collins

An Imprint of HarperCollins Publishers

YOU CAN'T WIN A FIGHT WITH YOUR CLIENT. Copyright ©
2007 by Tom Markert. All rights reserved. Printed in the
United States of America. No part of this book may be
used or reproduced in any manner whatsoever without
written permission except in the case of brief quotations
embodied in critical articles and reviews. For information,
address HarperCollins Publishers, 10 East 53rd Street,
New York, NY 10022.

HarperCollins books may be purchased for educational,
business, or sales promotional use. For information, please
write: Special Markets Department, HarperCollins Publishers, 10 East 53rd Street, New York, NY 10022.

FIRST EDITION

Designed by Joy O'Meara

Markert, Tom.
  You can't win a fight with your client & 49 other rules
for providing great service / Tom Markert. —1st ed.
        p. cm.
  ISBN-10: 0–06–122855–9
  ISBN-13: 978–0–06–122855–1
  1. Customer services.   2. Customer relations.   3.
Customer satisfaction.   4. Success in business.   I. Title.
  HF5415.5.M166   2007
  658.8'12   dc22

06 07 08 09 10 ID/RRD 10 9 8 7 6 5 4 3 2 1

This book is dedicated to real basketball people who have played a role in my life:

Don Bligh: Ninth grade, Chittenango High School
Dan Kinsella: JV, Chittenango High School
Phil Gordon: Varsity, Chittenango High School
Mike Seymour: JV, St. Lawrence University
Paul Evans: Varsity, St. Lawrence University
Lee Talbot: Varsity, St. Lawrence University
Emmett Davis: Varsity, Colgate University, U.S. Naval Academy
Brian Goorjian and Billy Tomlinson: Sydney Kings
Shane Heal: Melbourne South Dragons
Rick Burton: NBL Australia Commissioner
David Stern: NBA Commissioner

Thanks, guys. Your efforts mattered!

CONTENTS

INTRODUCTION

A few years back, savvy marketers reached the conclusion that the next new thing was to conquer the universe. And to conquer the universe you had to be big. You had to have scale. That's how merger mania and the acquisition craze started in the mid–1990s.

And the race to get big was on! Food companies gobbled up food companies. Retailers bought up other retailers. Banks cashed in by buying other banks. Others, such as Wal-Mart, just grew rapidly on their own. The message was clear as a bell: Surviving, let alone thinking, as a small operation wasn't going to be easy. Size and scale can be a formidable weapon. It gives you buying power and leverage, money to advertise, opportunities to offer sharper prices, and resources to bring products to market more quickly and efficiently.

So what does it mean? It means that there are lots of very big companies out there today. If your business is reliant on providing a service or supplying a product to any company, but particularly to a big company for a large stream of revenue, this could present both an opportunity and a threat. The opportunity to increase your revenue by providing excellent servicing to these companies is huge, but if you fail to service your big clients perfectly, you could very well lose that business to a hungry, aggressive competitor in a heartbeat. And losing is not good. Think of all you lose—not only the revenue but also the cost and time of trying to get the business back!

But servicing a client is hard work and should never be underestimated. Big clients, in particular, have upsides and downsides and therefore are generally managed at a different level inside most smart companies. Looking for a company's top servicing team? Look for those managing the biggest accounts in a company's portfolio.

In fact this was best exemplified when I asked the

CEO of one of the world's largest consumer products companies who was the most important person in their organization. Without hesitation, he shot back at me, "The gentleman who heads up our Wal-Mart team. They control more than forty percent of our total business right now. If we are not servicing them just right, and I mean just right, our business is dead. We can't cover a bad year at Wal-Mart elsewhere in the business. They are just so big. Our version of a rock star runs the Wal-Mart business."

In *You Can't Win a Fight with Your Client*, I gathered 50 rules regularly observed by some of the world's best client service companies and client service executives. I hope these rules guide you well as you manage a large account and teach you how to service all your clients like a pro.

Service, service, service!

RULE 1

Know Your Products

You can never be truly effective with a client if you do not have a solid understanding of your product portfolio and the full capabilities of your company. There is no shortcut or workaround on this one. Clients want their problems solved as fast and painlessly as possible. Your ability to supply a solution is critical. A superficial understanding of your products and their range of capabilities simply isn't good enough. For example, when a client says, "Here is where I need your help. Is this something that you do?" You can't answer, "I'm not sure. I'll get back to you." Why? Because the client will surely assume that even if you do offer a service that can help solve that particular problem, it must not be core to what you do or surely you would have known immediately. Credibility crusher!

Perhaps worse, not fully understanding your company's range of capabilities can cost your company dearly both in terms of immediate and long-term sales. Imagine if your company had a product or capability you were unaware of and thus failed to bring it to your client's attention. As a result, your client brought in a competitive supplier who did a great job on the project. You now have a problem or at least a worry you didn't need to have.

If you are running a large account, take the initiative to ensure that you and everyone who works for you is fully trained on all your products and offerings.

This sounds basic, but it isn't so easy in today's environment. Most companies have dramatically cut back on formal training programs that for many years were a staple in business.

This is not true in every business, however. If you read *Fortune* magazine's (January 23, 2007) list of the 100 best companies to work for in 2006, you would see that many companies offer 40-plus hours of training each year. But these are the exceptions and certainly not the norm in today's environment.

You may want to test your team or certify them in each area of your business. But let's face the truth. Learning your products and capabilities is basic in any business, and it takes personal initiative. It's not something you can delegate. It is something you have to want in your belly and something you are willing to go for. The fact that your company does not make training broadly available can't be used as an excuse.

Chase product knowledge because it will pay dividends.

RULE 2

Never Bad-Mouth Competition

Almost every industry today involves multiple competitors, and yours is probably not the exception. Every competitor has some point of differentiation or, stated another way, a reason for being. It's important to know their product line as well as you know yours so that you can effectively sell the benefits that your offering provides in the context of what else is available.

But remember that you never win over a

client by trash-talking a competitor. You win contracts by effectively selling your own products and services. And, of course, by selling yourself. Clients almost never buy things from people they don't like. Think about it. When was the last time that you bought something from someone you disliked or who had bad-mouthed someone else? Not anytime recently, I bet.

Professional servicing requires you to always stay on very high ground. You can effectively communicate your advantages to a client without ever belittling a competitor.

RULE 3

Understand Revenue and Profit Targets

Your primary job is for the company you work for. The trick is always in balancing the needs of your employer and the sometimes overwhelming needs of your clients. A critical first step toward that is to be intimately acquainted with the revenue and profit targets you have been assigned by your company.

So many account managers I have encountered have little or no understanding of the financials of the accounts they manage. I hate it when I hear "I'll do everything I can for my client and just see how the numbers turn out." No, no, no. You need to own your numbers and understand every single detail about them.

There is an old saying in many service companies: "Mix matters." You have an obligation to do everything you can to get the numbers to land just where they were set to land by your company. The reason is simple. Each component of your business likely has a different profit contribution, which means that if you are not careful, you might sell lots of low-profit items and reach your volume goals but miss your overall profit goal!

It is important for you to achieve your overall number but equally important that you get there by following your company's expectations. You can do that only if you know your numbers cold.

It has been my observation that most people in the servicing game are more qualitative than quantitative. Translation . . . they go for the softer skills versus math skills . . . which makes sense. But truly good client service folks need to be proficient in both areas. Both the soft skills and the business math skills are easily learned with a bit of effort and some practice.

Don't be embarrassed to ask for help if you are uncomfortable. A few good questions later and you will fully understand your business and financial objectives.

RULE 4

Know Contract Details

One thing I have learned over the years is that clients will always throw a contract in front of you if the terms and conditions of that contract favor them. But if a client wants something and it's not in the contract, there will be no mention of the contract. Surprise, surprise, surprise.

It amazes me how many times people managing a large account fail to fully understand the details of the contract between their company and the client. Carefully reading through the contract only makes good business sense. The contract is the bond between the two companies. It is the document that outlines what your company is being paid to deliver. It is what was promised. It is what you will be judged against.

On day 1 of your assignment, read the contract thoroughly and fully understand what is included and what is not included in the deal. Find out from the contract what your company agreed to provide and compare that with what your company is providing today. Meet with your legal counsel and get their interpretations if necessary.

Business relationships have a life beyond the contract. Over time, the client's needs and your capabilities shift, which means that you often end up providing some things that are in the contract and some that are not. It also means that you may not be providing other things you had agreed to provide. It's pretty common in business. It's all about balance and fulfilling the spirit of the contract. But as relationships and commitment shift, the contract should be modified to reflect the changes.

You should never let a contract get out of date. Make changes, create addendums, but keep the contract current.

_____

RULE 5

Take Advantage of Being the New Guy

A lesson that I learned early on in my career with Procter & Gamble had to do with taking advantage of being the new guy. You only get to play this card once—only at the beginning of your relationship with a client. It is a clever tactic and worth adopting if you can. It plays out like this: You are new to your assignment. Human nature being what it is, almost everyone feels a bit sorry for the new guy and wants to be helpful in the early days. It's a unique time in a relationship and one that you should fully leverage. Ask questions. Have the client give you history lessons on the business. Ask what needs to be improved. Ask what is not right. You have one shot at this, but it is the single best opportunity you will ever have to learn everything in a friendly environment and get off to a fast start with a new client.

You can use the new-guy status for about a year. It gives you license to make mistakes, ask questions, and simply feel your way around. It's always worked for me!

RULE 6

Know Your Client's Objectives

Knowing your client's objectives sounds easy, but it isn't. You would think clients would be transparent about their business objectives with a business partner, but you couldn't be more wrong. Clients often closely guard information from suppliers.

As a good and clever supplier, you must sort through a plan for best obtaining your client's most critical objectives. The simplest starting place is with your main contact point. Ask him or her to make time to walk through these objectives with you. Ask questions and make sure you have clarity. If you have deeper contacts, verify with them the accuracy of the objectives from their point of view. Read the annual report if available (more on that later). Do an Internet search and read everything that's currently being written about the company and anyone who works at the company.

The point of all this is that there is seldom one set of objectives for a client. Individuals add their own flavor to corporate objectives all the time. If you don't invest the effort in getting the objectives down and setting your action plan for contributing to those objectives, you have lost. You have given the client no decent way of benchmarking your success—no quantitative method to prove your value.

RULE 7

Read the Annual Report

If you don't already make a practice of reading your client's annual report, you certainly should. A company's annual report is a declaration document. It details financial performance and offers predictions. It lays out key priorities, strategies, opportunities, and direction. If you've ever wanted to learn what senior executives at your client's organization are thinking about ... the annual report is the way to do it!

Reading the annual report will help you

tie your efforts to your client's strategic plans. Strategic plans don't change often. Let's face it: A radical change in strategic direction from one annual report to the next—absent some disruptive event—would be a bit odd!

So read the annual report cover to cover. If you get stuck on the financials, that's okay. Most people do. Ask one of the finance people in your company to walk you through them. You will have a chance to meet someone new at your company, and they will love doing hands-on client work.

RULE 8

Establish Key Performance Indicators

When you are running a large account, it is very important that you establish key performance indicators, or KPIs, as they are commonly known.

KPIs are a straightforward way of establishing an agreement on what your client needs and what you are committing to do for that client during the course of a year or a mutually agreed-on period of time. Make no mistake, establishing KPIs for a large client is not easy. Often you will have many contacts inside a client company, each of whom requires your time and attention. Inventory everyone who will judge your performance and find out what they need from you. More important, find out what you must do for them to feel that you've serviced them successfully.

As you are analyzing the input you've collected, be conscious of the people who provided feedback. Ask yourself who the most important people are in the client company. As in every company, there is a pecking order. Weigh the responses of those of greater influence a bit more heavily. Once you collect all this information, the trick is then to condense it into a meaningful and measurable document. My advice . . . keep it simple. This is not an area in which you want any complications to creep in.

Once you have a draft of the KPIs, ask yourself if you and your company can accomplish everything on the list. You should strive to set stretch goals but commit only to goals that you believe have a reasonable probability of being achieved.

Finally, review your KPIs with key stake-holders in the client company. Get their final agreement and sign off on the objectives. Set a series of review dates (no less than quarterly), and in those meetings clearly talk about your and your company's achievements and also any areas that might need corrections.

You cannot become complacent about this step. Clients get busy, you get busy, and before long, these meetings slip right up to the point of the end of the contract. There is no worse time to review progress! It's too late at that point if anything has gone wrong.

Clients like KPIs. They make them feel in control of the relationship and raise their confidence in both you and your company. Make setting and reviewing KPIs a reality.

RULE 9

Offer a Total Solution

Answering a client's specific question is always a good thing, and sometimes it is enough. But often in today's business environment, the question you answer may be only the tip of the iceberg for a client. The truly good service professionals are always focused on doing everything possible to bring complete solutions to clients. When a client raises a question or asks for help, they don't just take it on face value—they probe, dig, and think outside the box to do more than just answer the question at hand.

Servicing is very competitive. Solutions for clients are often complex. The professional who brings simplicity and total solutions is always the winner!

Tom Markert

RULE 10

Be a Client Advocate

Being excellent at running a large account requires you to be a strong advocate for your client. Why? All clients are not treated the same. Big clients are often treated differently from small clients. They have more clout and more money to experiment, to try new things, and to seek new and innovative solutions. They are prestigious and can take their business partners to a whole new level. Big clients are hard to get and harder to keep. And these big clients want the single best account managers that they can get their hands on. Why? It's simple: The account manager drives success or failure with a client. He or she is the quarterback who orchestrates all the plays. Account managers direct resources and get senior management to pay extra attention to their accounts.

If you run a large account for your company, you must learn to become a tremendous advocate for your client. Keep management 100% up to speed on developments with your client, both good and bad, and actively engaged with the activities of the client. Seek ways to help the client find better service. Get them involved in pilot programs that your company may be running. Push the envelope of possibilities. Elevate your client to new heights. Find ways to differentiate them and make them feel special.

All clients like that. Large clients demand that.

Deliver on Your Promise

Do what you promised you would do! Solid words to live by.

Clients crave consistency. Clients want to work with people they trust and people who deliver. If you make a promise, you must do everything that you can to deliver on that promise. It is your word, your bond. Good client work is all about setting stretch targets and objectives and then chipping away at them each and every day until you meet them—every one of them—and on time.

Clients gain faith slowly and loose faith quickly. An occasional missed promise will often be overlooked if your track record has been solid. A series of mistakes or missed promises, on the other hand, is the death knell for you. You won't succeed, and you will get asked off the project . . . and that's embarrassing.

If you make a promise, make sure you live up to it.

RULE 12

Build Relationships Everywhere

Personal relationships are critical in business. They always have been, and they always will be.

No matter what business or industry you compete in, you must make it job one to forge strong business relationships. Business relationships develop over time and only with very consistent and trustworthy servicing. Business relationships start with your very first meeting, arguably your most important meeting! In the first meeting, set the tone for the relationship and lay a foundation of expectations. The relationship then begins to develop on the basis of your ability to deliver on the results the client is expecting. Each month of flawless delivery puts a penny in the bank. Each mistake takes 5 to 10 cents out, depending on its severity. Get the ratio? You get a little credit for doing things well yet crucified for every mistake! Mistakes matter!

No matter what your line of business, it is critical that you take the job of building relationships with your clients very seriously. Long gone are the days of having to worry about only one or two people inside a company. Decisions today get made by a large degree of consensus and often by committee. Having a strong relationship with one person may not be enough for you to hold on to an account. And trust me—if something goes wrong, you definitely want to have lots of friends.

Relationship-building is not easy. It takes multiple exposures. Relationships at the top of your client company are also critical. Getting to the C-level people—the top dogs, such as the chief executive officer (CEO), the chief marketing officer (CMO), and the chief financial officer (CFO)—is hard work. Getting to those folks and squeezing out 5 or 10 minutes to form a relationship, wow—really impossible ... but oh so critical. They can be your best friend or your worst enemy. They sit in a position from which they can override any decision in their company at any time.

And don't forget to make contact with the purchasing department. They are the new player in the mix. These professional negotiators get involved in all significant arrangements, and they can be a tough mob to deal with. They are trained to be exacting and relentless. Having some trust or relationship with them can only benefit you. They are often trained to avoid external relationships, so they may be toughest of all to get to know. My advice is to try really hard. Winning them over ups your chances of success dramatically.

RULE 13

Win Over Frosty

In every client relationship, you will certainly meet at least one individual who for some reason is frosty toward you. Maybe they do not like your service or product, or they favor a competitor, or they were mistreated by someone at your company. Maybe they just don't like you.

It doesn't matter. Work on them. Put a plan in place to win them over. Resist the urge to only spend time with those who are friendly—that's too easy! Frosty is a snake waiting in the woodpile ready to strike out. You must find a way to move Frosty from hostile to at least neutral. It may take a long time, but this is a problem not to be ignored, for it can cause irreparable damage.

I watched a colleague of mine, Audrey Rosen, who is now a vice president with Knowledge Networks, an online research company, work magic in this area years ago. The company that we were working for was trying desperately to renew our contract with Gillette. It was a big, important contract. The relationship was good overall, but our relationship with a key individual in the sales organization was frosty. He was influential. He was loud. He was not afraid to voice his opinions. We thought that he could derail us, and we had a few scant months to get our house in order.

Enter Audrey, who rose to the challenge of taking on the task of fixing that relationship. She met with him, listened to his issues, put plans and timelines in place to get things right. She built a trusting relationship with him, and while in three months he was not a fan, he had become neutral. He gave us a fair chance, and we delivered. Fast-forward: We won the account, and over time Frosty became an ally. That felt good!

What happens if you do not fix that relationship? I bet you lose.

RULE 14

Be Switzerland

Politics exist inside every client's organization, just as they do in your company. It is important to get a handle on your client's political hot spots as well as on who dislikes whom. Who gets along with whom? Who is politically dangerous? Friends or enemies? Opportunity or threat? And then remain as neutral as possible.

As a supplier, you must be Switzerland. You do not want to be seen as an ally to any particular camp. That will make you a target for others and limit your ability to be truly successful. Understand, however, that neutrality comes with a price. It makes gathering information harder and relationship-building more difficult and time-consuming. But in the long run, you can be far more successful at managing your client by being everyone's friend and not alienating any one person or a group of people in your client's organization.

RULE 15

Entertain Clients

I have always believed entertaining clients to be a good thing. Many big companies, however, have strict policies governing what is acceptable and what is not in this arena. Some companies, such as Wal-Mart, prohibit suppliers and service providers from entertaining their employees. Always understand and respect your client's entertainment policies, but whenever it is acceptable and possible, use entertainment as a means to further develop your business relationship with a client.

Entertainment can be a simple thing, such as going to a ball game or a lunch or dinner together. It doesn't have to be fancy, expensive, or lavish to be effective. Entertainment is a way to get a client out of the work environment, discuss some business, and further build relationships.

Keep your plans simple and modest. Keep the time commitment to a few hours. Do something your client likes to do and not necessarily something you like to do. Make it fun and low key.

RULE 16

Work On-Site

If you provide services in an industry in which working on-site (as opposed to just stopping in for a meeting) is possible, by all means do it.

Working on-site is the new-millennium answer to building meaningful relationships. It lets you "inside the kingdom." You'll get invited to meetings. You'll learn what your client is trying to achieve firsthand. You find out who's doing what for whom. Best of all, you'll meet everyone in your client organization—the first step in building a relationship. By working on-site, eventually you become an extension of the client's team. You see all the moving pieces, not just those that touch your business. Your ability to add value rises exponentially.

On-site servicing has become a staple in many industries, such as information companies and agencies. A version of on-site servicing has even flourished in retailing. Executives from hundreds of companies that supply or service Wal-Mart now live in Bentonville, Arkansas, right in Wal-Mart's backyard. They might not work on-site at Wal-Mart's headquarters, but they live in the same community as Wal-Mart's executives, and in some cases right next door. They worship with the same religious groups and go to the same Little League games. It's expensive to have a representative working so far from headquarters, but these suppliers and service organizations do it because it works.

Working on-site is not always easy to pull off. Establish a routine so that the experience is not so random to the client. For instance, you might make a point of working on-site every Friday. Whenever possible, get a dedicated office or cube with a phone and a line for your computer. While you are on-site, make sure that you are adding value. This means getting involved, rolling up your sleeves, and helping solve meaningful issues side by side with the client. It doesn't mean sitting at your desk, talking on the phone, or catching up on e-mails. In fact, I have witnessed clients disbanding on-site servicing when this occurred. Working on-site is a privilege, and you will be held to higher standards. Use the privilege carefully.

RULE 17

Go Coach Class

With clients, perception is reality. If you are traveling domestically with a client, always sit in economy class. Clients hate it when suppliers travel up front. They see the cost of your first-class tickets affecting the price they pay for your products and service—and they are right! The client is always right!

One more tip: Don't use upgrades when traveling with a client. You can turn blue in the face telling a client that you are using upgrades, and they still won't believe you.

International flights are always an exception. Fly business class or use upgrades, but avoid first class. As far as a client is concerned, you are sitting in first class and they pay your bills, so you are spending their money unwisely.

This rule also extends to anything that is visible to a client. I once had a boss who decided to buy a beautiful and expensive Mercedes-Benz. He wasn't a show-off or anything like that, but he did love cars. On the day he got the car, we had a meeting with Nestlé, who was a major client of ours at the time. We pulled up and parked in the visitor slot just as our key contact was pulling in. He came over and looked at the car and in a half-serious, half-joking way, said, "Geez, the margins on our contract must be pretty healthy!" You can see the point. Be careful of your image with all of your clients.

RULE 18

——

Get Invited to Meetings

It is very important to become ingrained in your clients' organization. Finding a way to be a part of their team and finding a way to bring real and meaningful value is what will set you and your organization apart from all the others who are trying and just not succeeding.

I have never been a big fan of meetings, but you can use meetings to your advantage. Find a way to get invited to the meetings that really matter and use these opportunities to find out the clients issues, problems, and hot spots. At these meetings, listen to the most senior managers very closely. Remember, they have the power. They set the direction for their company. They ultimately make the decisions, including the decision to keep your products or services and ultimately you yourself.

Also be prepared to contribute in meetings, really contribute. Zero in on an issue that you can own or make a big contribution on and ask to own it! No client ever turns down help or suggestions. Clients love help! The larger the contribution you make at these meetings, the more reliant the client becomes on you and your company. And reliance is the sweet spot of client service.

RULE 19

Practice Presentations

Delivering presentations is a commonplace occurrence inside most large companies these days. When preparing for a presentation take great care in assembling the material as well as practicing the presentation before you get in front of an audience.

Today, presentations are usually delivered with the help of PowerPoint slides. Most people fall into the trap of including every point of their presentation on the slides. Big mistake.

Keep your slides very clear and uncluttered. Know precisely what your message points are and hit them multiple times during the presentation. Short is better than long. This is a hard concept to grasp for some people! And don't forget: The summary and recommendations slide is the most important slide of your presentation and thus you should put significant effort into it. This is the "everlasting image" slide . . . the one they remember.

Smart account managers often review their presentation with someone from the client company before a meeting. This could alert you to any land mines in your presentation and maybe point you in a direction you had not considered. This is a really clever step but requires great planning. It means getting the presentation done on a tighter schedule so that you have time to make this happen.

Presentations are like theater in many ways. The audience wants to be entertained. They want to see a great performance as a result of hours of hard work. They want to be happy at the end. Perfection comes with practice.

RULE 20

Communicate

Communication is critical in every relationship, and that holds very true for successfully managing a large account.

As I have said earlier, when working with a client, you seldom have one master. You have many, and it's very important that you communicate with all of them regularly. Tailor your message to each individual or group, and be mindful of how you communicate it. The style of communication often must be

adjusted for the particular person you are trying to reach.

Sales speaks a different language from
marketing. Finance, a different language from
research. To be truly effective, you do have to
learn to be a chameleon (in a good way). You
have to change your skin colors to blend in
to your surroundings or, in this case, to better
relate to the audience you are speaking to or
working with.

Communication should not be done ran-
domly. Instead, it should be consistent, well
thought out, and thorough. Communicate your
progress against objectives regularly. But don't
be too obnoxious about it. Do it in a confident
and proud way. Praise the members of your
team who drove the success as well as folks on
the client side who contributed to the projects.
The more you can align your team and its success with the client's success, the better.

RULE 21

Call with "No News"

Often it takes days or weeks to answer a question that a client may pose. Nothing wrong with that, but in the interim between when the question is asked and when the answer is available, it is important to keep the client updated or simply to call and say, "I have not forgotten about your question, and we should have an answer soon." The fact that you take a couple of minutes to call demonstrates that you care about the client and are dedicated to your job.

This is a gesture that will take only a few seconds but will have a lasting impact on your relationship with your client.

RULE 22

Answer Your Phone

You can delegate authority, but you can't delegate responsibility. Clients expect fast turnaround on everything you give them. Frankly, they pay the bills, and they deserve it.

When a client calls, pick up the phone! In the age of mobile phones and mobile e-mail devices, everyone should be instantly reachable during most business hours. If you are managing an account, keep your phone on except when you are meeting with others. It's simply rude to pick up your cell phone (unless it is an emergency) when you are meeting with an individual or a group. Don't waste time screening calls. Don't you hate waiting for a call to be returned? Don't you love it when someone picks up the phone and solves your problem? Sometimes voice mail is unavoidable, but you must always return a client's call by close of business, even if it's to say you have no new news.

Be smart about letting clients know your whereabouts. If you are traveling, leave that information on your voice-mail message. Same goes for your e-mail. Turn on the "out of office" feature and update it with your whereabouts and how often you will likely have access to your mail. It's always best if a client knows your availability. It helps level expectations.

RULE 23

Give Out Your Phone Number

Rarely will clients call you outside of business
hours. People are mostly courteous, after all.
Nonetheless, always give your client your full
and complete contact details.

Give them your office number, your mobile
number, your home number, and your e-mail
address. If you're going on vacation, give them
your hotel number and a fax number. All of
this is standard operating procedure with many
consulting giants. At the beginning of each cli-

ent engagement, they provide you with a sheet listing full and complete contact details for every member of the team. It positions them as very professional and always available during an engagement period.

Trust me—clients call only if there's a dire emergency. But the simple and meaningful gesture of passing over your contact details signals that you care and that you are deeply committed to them and their organization.

Following this rule is an easy way to score big points.

RULE 24

Stick to Your Allotted Time

To effectively service a client, you have to professionally manage each interaction that you have with members of a client's organization. Specifically, you must manage the amount of time you spend with every person and client.

Clients appreciate promptness. It shows respect and professionalism and demonstrates commitment. Running over on a meeting time is never a good thing. Most clients are fully scheduled each and every day. A late meeting can have a domino effect on their day and quite possibly disrupt their entire schedule. Not a good reflection on you.

Start every meeting with a client by confirming the purpose of the meeting and the amount of time allocated for the meeting. Stick to the agenda unless the client insists the meeting go another way. Watch your time carefully while going through each item on your agenda. Wrap up on time, including handling any last-minute questions.

This is a small thing, is easy to do, and really matters.

RULE 25

Respect Your Client

It is very important that you always treat your clients with the utmost respect. Of course from time to time clients may not deserve your respect, but always give it to them without fail. If they disrespect you, swallow your pride, quell your anger, control your temper, and act like a true professional. Unwavering respect of your client will win every day and in the long run.

Once you start down a path of showing dis-respect toward your clients, you have taken the first step toward losing them. It's a disastrous path and one to be avoided at all costs.

RULE 26

You Can't Win a Fight with Your Client

You can't win a fight with your client. Sound stupid? Perhaps, but I see account managers trying to win fights with their clients all the time. It is the proverbial kiss of death.

Clients generally don't mind if you have a competing point of view on a topic. And a smart client will welcome different thinking on a subject. That said, you do need to remember the pecking order—and you are not the bird with the biggest beak! When a client is clearly making an argument in one direction and is clearly not going to move off that position, it is time to give in and align with his or her decision.

Fighting with your client is never a good thing. Once you cross the line with a client, your relationship will suffer permanent damage. In extreme cases, your client might be angry enough that they will actually ask not to work with you on a project.

Never let your emotions run high with your client. You can't win every point, and you certainly can't win a fight with your client.

RULE 27

Accept Criticism

As an account manager, you will never do everything right—although striving for that is a great goal. Clients tend to criticize. It is just something they seem to do. So my advice is: Don't fight it at all. Accept that from time to time you will be criticized, sometimes openly and sometimes very politely, with venting done behind closed doors. Accept whatever criticism comes your way clinically and without emotion. It doesn't really matter how you got the information. What matters is what you do with it. After all, criticism is little more than feedback on your performance.

Probe what you are being told extensively. Make sure that you understand it and are in a position to make the changes necessary to get back on the right track. It is important that you do react quickly and keep the person who offered the criticism updated on your plans to improve and on the progress toward making any necessary changes. Clients feel good when suppliers listen and correct bad situations.

RULE 28

Speak the Truth

It has been my experience that you never get hurt in the long run by speaking the truth. The truth always wins . . . particularly with clients.

Clients want trust from their partners. They want to know that they can believe everything they are told by you and your company. And why not? They make decisions on the basis of the information you provide, and their careers hang in the wind when they make a decision based on a falsehood. Get caught in one direct lie, and trust me—you will be asked off the project. You can correct most mistakes, but you cannot correct a lie with a client.

I am always reminded of the great quote attributed to Marion Barry, ex-mayor of Washington, D.C.: "There are two kinds of truth. There are real truths and made-up truths." Well, in the business of client service, unlike in politics, there is only one truth.

———————————————————————

RULE 29

Make the Best Out
of Bad Situations

Every business has dark days, and how a company handles a dark day is largely defined by how quickly and sincerely it acts to correct mistakes. Often, making small gestures of goodwill clearly demonstrate sincerity. Simple acts can diffuse gravely difficult situations in any business.

Think about it. When you are sitting on a plane that is stuck on a tarmac because of a snowstorm, does it help if the pilot routinely gives you an update, or do you like to be kept in the dark? Does it help if the flight attendants pass out pillows and blankets and something to drink, or does doing nothing make sense?

Similarly, when things go wrong with a client, find ways to mitigate the pain—and do it quickly. People can't get too mad if they know you are making the very best of a bad situation. Timely communication and updates are always critical.

RULE 30

Never Give Up Your Company

If something goes wrong on your watch, never ever blame your company or another coworker. Clients hate excuses and see right through them anyway. So don't waste your breath. Don't say "The company screwed up" or "Sally in the factory screwed up." It cheapens you and the company that you work for. What the client will hear is that you think you were flawless but that your company or your coworker stinks. The client will hear you passing the buck or blaming someone else and basically shirking any responsibility.

Be direct. Tell the client a mistake was made and that it's being corrected. Issue resolved!

RULE 31

—

Don't Embarrass the Client

Clients make mistakes—sometimes big and sometimes often. Occasionally a client's mistake will negatively affect your ability to deliver on an objective. But calling out a client's mistake is never a winning strategy.

I have found it's always best to not blame a client or an individual at a client company for your inability to deliver on your promise. The individual you blame will never forgive you, and you will make an enemy for life—never a good idea. On the other hand, your not pointing fingers at anyone will make the individual who dropped the ball feel indebted to you, which could lead to an even better relationship with that person.

Admit that a mistake was made and blame no one. People usually forgive those who say, "I'm sorry."

Focus on fixing the problem, not on who caused the problem, particularly if that someone is a client!

RULE 32

Respect Confidentiality

As you work closely with a client and gain their trust, you will over time be exposed to more and more confidential information. This additional confidential information almost always will allow you to do your job better, which is great for you as an individual and great for the company you work for.

Any breach of confidentiality on your part, however, will come with a sudden and steep price. Passing on confidential information without the permission of the person who trusted you is not an option. If something is said to you in confidence, you must remain silent about that information. Remember that you cannot recover from a mistake in this area. Once you have breached confidentiality with a client, that client will no longer trust you. In fact, by your breaching that trust, it's very possible that you may have put that client in an awkward situation and possibly even jeopardized their job.

Treat any confidential information as sensitive, and you will never find yourself apologizing to a client for a grave mistake.

RULE 33

Learn Whom You Can Trust

In every relationship there are people you can trust and people you can't. The same holds true for clients. Trust is an element of a relationship that is built over time and is the result of consistently positive behavior.

In time you must determine who it is at the client organization that you can truly trust. Whom can you talk to in confidence? Whom can you gather information from, and with whom can you share your issues and concerns? To whom can tell you the truth about what is really going behind the scenes at the client site? This is information you need, and it's often not readily volunteered. Once you have determined whom you can trust and, conversely, once that person at the client's organization completely trusts *you*, you can position yourself to receive that stream of confidential and critical information.

RULE 34

Educate Your Owner

Often clients just don't know how to make themselves look good. I've seen it time and time again—clear instances in which the main contact person or handler at a client organization isn't smart at all about how they manage their partners or suppliers. They often pick apart their partner after a small mistake, forgetting that they too are judged on how well the relationship performs. Smart handlers don't allow that to happen—they work to ward off any negativity, as they recognize that it's a direct reflection on them.

If as an account manager you find yourself in a position in which your handler at the client organization does not appear to be protective and caring, find a quiet way to let them know how important your relationship is. Just let them know you need their help. Casually mention that you know they have a personal stake in achieving a successful partnership. Perhaps even recount how a good two-way relationship actually works.

Never be afraid of leveling with or coaching a client. So much of your future is tied to them.

I caught up with Randy Stone, who is now the president of MMA, a servicing company involved in data modeling and consulting for Fortune 500 companies. Randy has always been one of the best involved in servicing clients that I've witnessed. I asked him simply, "How do you do so well with clients?" He said it was not magic but education for those he worked with. "I am not afraid to level set the relationship at the very start. I always tell my clients the same thing. First, in a public forum we present a unified stance working toward a common goal. Behind closed doors, with no witnesses, you can criticize me all you want. Second, as a client you want to be viewed by my people as the best business to work on and not a nightmare client. Why? Because then you get the best people asking to work on your business. Third, let's both agree to be open on feedback. You tell me what you think and allow me to voice what I'm thinking. Fourth, and most important, we are stronger working together. Let's never forget that. If the client and I agree on these terms . . . life is good!"

You might want to steal these ideas.

RULE 35

Never Say No

When managing a client, it is important to remember that your clients are always right . . .
even when they are wrong.

Clients make requests all the time. They
sometimes make outrageous requests or requests that you can't deliver on. But you should
never ignore a client's request, hoping that they
will magically forget. They won't. But when a
client asks for something you can't do, never
say no. Instead, give thought to what you can

do to solve that client's problem in a different way. Even if you can't do exactly what the client wants, there's always an alternative that might fit the bill. In the worst case, if the client doesn't accept your alternative, offering one demonstrates that you care and that you are trying hard. That counts with clients.

Some will debate me on the merits of saying no to a client. Saying no is clear. The word *no* wipes out any ambiguity. But in a professional servicing environment, saying no doesn't help a client think through alternatives. In my experience, people like to be helped when they come to you with a problem. I know I do. If I go to a hardware store and need something and they don't have exactly what I want, then I want them to make another recommendation. Works for me.

I think it's always best to offer an alternative. If it's not a viable option, the client will let you know, probably thank you, and then move on.

Who likes to be told no anyway?

RULE 36

Find Ways to Make Their Lives Easier

Get to know as much as you can about your client and find a way to make their lives easier. Pick a task close to your line of work and offer to grab it for your client. It doesn't have to be something that you promise to do for them permanently—just offer to do it once in a while. To the client it shows initiative and demonstrates a clear interest in their business. It separates you from competitors who are too lazy or too stupid to think about helping out.

Get to really know your client and pitch in!

RULE 37

Make Recommendations

Clients are like everyone else. They want their lives made easier. They pay you a fee, and as a part of that fee, they expect you to bring them solutions. Solutions require you to take a stand and become intimately familiar with your client's business, and they require confidence and courage.

This is the stuff that separates the boys from the men, and the girls from the women. Clients love to have suppliers make intelligent recommendations. Making intelligent recommendations will elevate you in the eyes of the client. It will allow you to command a premium for your service if you get yourself in a position in which you are so knowledgeable that you can add value at a much higher level than your competitors.

Now, it's not easy to be in a position to make an intelligent recommendation. You have to know a lot about a client's business before you can go out on a limb. After all, you don't want to make a stupid recommendation. But don't be shy.

RULE 38

Empower Clients with Self-Sufficiency

In all industries, clients want things fast, fast, and fast. Who can blame them? Getting things in real time means that they can compete in today's high-pressure business climate. Speed is a formidable advantage when it is used properly.

The best way to give them speed is to provide them access to the information they want, 24/7, 365 days a year. If they want a quick answer, they should be able to get it without having to pick up a phone and ask for it.

Of course this has different applications in different industries, but the underlying principle is the same.

That said, you must offer the solution in a way that is easy to use for your client and does not frustrate them in any way. Self-sufficiency works only if you make it easy and if people can get comfortable with the tools.

In recent history we have seen some great examples of self-sufficiency leading to commercial advantage. Look at automated teller machines. Who actually sees a teller anymore? How about self check-in at airports? Wow, that is way better than standing in long lines!

Clients like self-sufficiency if it is done properly.

RULE 39

Do the Unexpected

Everyone loves when someone does something extra nice for them—clients in particular!

Doing the unexpected for your client can come in many forms: analyzing an extra set of data, making a recommendation that shows great insight, helping to resolve a problem unrelated to the services you typically provide. These little or big unexpected gestures go beyond your client's expectations and set you apart from your competition.

RULE 40

Don't Be Afraid to Sell

Funny as it may sound, companies have come to devalue the word *sales*. It's no longer cool to say you are trying to sell something. Why? I don't know. After all, all companies are selling something—selling is what makes businesses go! No reason at all to be anything but damn proud if the word *sales* is in your job description.

Still, there has been a shift in how businesses buy services—and it should correspond with a shift in how you sell your services or products. Most buyers today are very thoughtful about their purchases, and the bigger the contract, the longer the process is and, of course, the greater the number of people involved in the decision.

Thus, the high-pressure days of "you must close the sale *now*" are over. Selling has become more professional as business has matured. Selling in some industries has become very "consultative," requiring a different kind of salesperson with a different skill set.

In the past, a good salesperson was capable of building relationships very quickly and sustaining them over time. While relationships remain very critical in selling today, they are not a sustainable method for consistently closing sales. Buyers are much more sophisticated and thoughtful than ever before. They want solutions from trusted providers—companies and people. They want to feel safe and assured. They want long-term relationships. It may take many individuals from a company carefully orchestrated to make a large sale at a large company. So the successful salesperson of to-day must be multiskilled and willing to work on a team.

Selling is fun! And it isn't a dirty word!

RULE 41

Learn From Those Who Are Doing It Well

Almost always, you can identify another company that conducts business with your client who has elevated the supplier–client relationship to a different level. It may be one of your client's big or small partners. Either way, find out who they are and what magic they are bringing to the party.

In fact, it might be a clever move to ask your client to identify who they would rate as their best business partner. They'll usually tell you. If the business partner is not competitive with your company, ask the client to arrange a meeting with them on your behalf. The client will love that you are seeking ways to become a better supplier, and you may unlock some great information from another supplier that you can use to improve your results.

RULE 42

Know Other Key Suppliers

In the business world, it has never been more important than it is today to find ways to work with the client's other key business suppliers. IBM refers to this as the "open ecosystem," a world where they will find a way to work with anyone to help solve a client's problem . . . even if that means working with a direct competitor.

I think it's a very good idea to get to know your client's other strategic business partners and get to know them well. Learn about their products and certainly meet their key people. You should explore possibilities on behalf of your mutual client or clients. You should discuss what obstacles might exist in a relationship and work to resolve them. Clients hate it when a good idea comes up and it takes forever for two suppliers to resolve their commercial issues. They don't care about the issues. They just want it done now. This is an area where being proactive with a client's other suppliers can score points. Get ahead of the game where you can. It can put you in a different spot from your competitors.

By the way, let your clients know that you are making the extra effort to get to know their other business partners.

RULE 43

Get Sticky

We all know the high costs associated with losing a client and the even higher costs of reacquiring a lost client. Retaining your clients is thus mission critical. Being sticky requires a lot of work, but it helps you retain clients.

I stole the term *sticky* from my friends at McKinsey. Getting sticky is all about entangling yourself at the client company through a myriad of spider webs. When you have become a critical link in a vast array of your client's projects, your client will find it hard to make a change or move away from your product or service. Getting sticky means that your client will suffer a high level of pain if they choose to unplug your company and plug in a competitor.

Figure out what would make you sticky with your client. Make a list of potential "sticky" possibilities. Work with your teammates and knock off those possibilities one at a time. Hey, a novel idea—ask your client how you can get sticky. I bet they will tell you.

RULE 44

Collect Advanced Intelligence

Constantly find new information and bring new ideas to your client. Stay on top of emerging trends and think about how they might benefit your client. Make suggestions, condense information for them, and freely share any intelligence you might have with them.

To collect this advanced intelligence for your clients, use every source at your disposal without violating any confidences. Ask industry experts. Ask peers in the industry what they are doing and thinking about. Ask your colleagues and friends who are business thought leaders. Build up a network of experts whom you can consult on a regular basis. Life is give and take. Eventually those experts will call you and ask for help.

The point is to reach beyond what is traditionally available to you or what is easy to find or get at. Gold nuggets aren't easy to find. Getting them takes hard work, but they are extraordinarily valuable. So is a piece of intelligence that you have that no one else does.

RULE 45

Ask for Help When You Need It

If you are tackling a big project for your client and it gets over your head, bring in the pros from Dover—people who have more subject-matter expertise than you do. You should never feel ashamed or intimidated about seeking help. It happens in the medical field all the time. For example, a general practitioner treats an illness or injury to only a certain point and then passes the baton to a specialist with a deep but narrow range of expertise. It's the same in business.

Everyone has limitations on expertise. No one is an expert in everything. Ask for help when you need it.

RULE 46

Roll Up Your Sleeves

There is no work that is beneath anyone. If a project needs to get done for a client and there is no one at the right level to do it, then roll up your sleeves and tackle it yourself.

Jumping in on a project or task that is not yours demonstrates leadership and commitment. Your staff will see you doing it and will take in a valuable lesson. And of course the client will have a better experience with the company because the work got done. Everyone comes up a winner.

RULE 47

Showcase Success

Clients are always busy, that's a fact. When managing a large account, you must always remember that it is very important to merchandise your accomplishments with all key stakeholders. Merchandising your success is not grandstanding, bragging, or showing off. It's simply letting the client know what you have done in the past and what you are capable of doing. Keeping the client apprised of what you are up to is simply a smart part of business life.

For years I've watched a colleague who is the unabashed master of merchandising his success. He sets an agenda that is realistic and each week delivers to his client a brilliant assessment of how his team is doing. Oh boy, does he sell success. In fact, he sells it so beautifully that every one of his clients thinks he's the best. When it is time to renew the client's contract, we never worry. His clients would never risk losing him!

Another master of merchandising success—and perhaps the single best operator I've ever witnessed in this area—is Bob McCann, currently the president of Nielsen Media Research International, who told me: "Pain is more easily remembered than pleasure. I wanted my clients to absolutely remember the good things, and talking about it routinely made it much more real. I talked about partnership, and I constantly told the clients how proud that I was of our track record in bringing value to the client. But nothing made me prouder than when my biggest client, Kraft, took out an ad in a newspaper in Green Bay to very publicly thank my team in that area of the country for outstanding work. I knew we had things just right at that moment."

RULE 48

Keep the Internal Team Updated

You should not lose site of the fact that often
many folks from your organization are involved
in servicing a client—some very directly and
some only tangentially. But many times these
people are operating in narrow silos, doing their
job but likely not very aware of all the other
contributions being made by the larger team.
Don't let this happen. Your teammates should
know what is going on at a client company at
all times. It helps them connect their contri-

butions with your client and, if nothing else, it raises their morale and energy. If you are running an account, make time to keep your team updated and well informed!

RULE 49

Go Home When the Job Is Done

The saying "Go home when the job is done" is true in any business. Every day there is a certain amount of work that needs to get done. The work can be internal work or client work; if you are doing your job right, you will know what that work is.

When you are managing a client, it is essential that your client work never fall behind. Falling behind is the kiss of death with a client. Establish a work plan and share it openly with your team and the clients. Stick to it and get the work done. Don't allow yourself to get distracted.

The old motto is true; go home when the work is done—and not one minute before.

RULE 50

Exude Quiet Confidence

The most successful client service executives always seem to possess the simplest quality: quiet confidence. They are not loud or arrogant. They are not mean; they are even-tempered. They are steady and sure-handed. They bring passion and energy to their work. They are undeterred in the face of difficulty. They may want to scream, but they never do. They don't hate problems; they love solving them.

Great servicing occurs when you truly love the game of servicing and have the confidence to get the job done with authority and grace.

ACKNOWLEDGMENTS

There are so many people to thank!

First of all, I would like to thank my wife, Sarah. She keeps the world moving! And my kids, Zach, Abby, Nate, and Rebecca. And a special thanks to my parents, Tom and Monnie Markert. I could never ask for more encouragement.

I would also like to thank various thought leaders who contributed to my thinking, including Randy Stone, Bob McCann, Ted Marzilli, Laurence Michael, Neil Preddy, Mike Keating, Audrey Rosen, Steve

Schmidt, Chris Kilbane, Chris Cody, Lucia Oddo, David McCallum, Rick Burton, Mike Whelan, John Bosarge, Bob Gardner, Jane Perrin, Ernesto Santos, Pete Palmer, Pam Maltby, Caryn Rae, Susan Moon, and Ed Markert, and Wendy Miller.

Thank you also to Faye Hicks, who diligently corrected my mistakes and kept me on time.

Last, thanks to the great team at HarperCollins, which includes Brian Murray, Marion Maneker, Genoveva Llosa, Beth Mellow, Sarah Brown, Angie Lee, Nyamekye Waliyaya, William Ruoto, and Vivian Gomez.